VIBES, KNIVES AND THIRSTS

"I am really so impressed by your poetry. Profound, powerful and much more!"
- Kirsten Westholter

"There is so much depth and vulnerability in the poems. It shows you really reached deep to write such words"
- Kemi Adegbola

"You are truly talented and the way you write poetry, it enables the reader to visualize the meaning of your words. It touches different people on so many levels."
- Anita Roberts

"when life filled my eyes to capacity with salty tears
and the road ahead still looked endless, my energy
resolved to use its filaments to feel the surrounding **vibes,**
their long edges became my **knives**
as I voyaged to my cravings **and thirsts"**

ISBN 979-8-9897163-0-2

VIBES, KNIVES AND THIRSTS

JOHN OLUGBENGA
OLOMOLEHIN

love is a very fearful island

housing a paradise within its core

and it's a paradise, housing frightening

fears within its core,

depending on where we see as the

entrance and the exit

the effects of various wars on my heart

have left it to shake terribly even if the

subtle touch on it is a knock from an angel

is it not an act of love and loyalty to ignore

common sense and mute the instinct just

because some manipulations are already

arranged to take place and there's an

essential need to act fooled

whenever gods and humans argue, the

gods are always the ones to go quiet first

and leave the table for their closets, to set

up some actions in the universe just to

prove their points because humans

arguments are like itchy bruises on the

body of the gods

the tests of life that i passed by guesswork

always return

the way you lured me into that sin

was the reason i accepted it

i still use the old hymns, references and
slangs from the religion i abandoned, for
the new god i found, but he always
bypasses those salutations and heads
straight to my heart for assessment and
conduct the business of the day

i will not withdraw from experiencing a
further intensity of dispensing love just for
the fear of the heart getting broken again

there's a price attached to who we say we

are that we always struggle to pay

everything that took me away from what i

loved to do, stood side by side like a

bunch of sympathizers who heard a

certain thunderous cry for help but

wouldn't leave their posts to render any

after putting in all the efforts i could

assemble, i realised that the exact time

which the universe wanted to make me a

hero was far from the dates i picked and

planned to become one myself

the energy i attract is always two-faced,
and i've come to believe that one beckons
to the other after seeing the size of the
room i put up in me for rent

if you run away from love, the first escape

will take you to the ridges of land that

demarcate lakes of smaller love, then you'll

reach an open field where everything

looks

free but not, it is just the luring surface of

a gravitational pull towards the love for

something or someone else

and who do we ask for peace, do we

beseech the gods or the government

or ignore both and just reshuffle the

elements within us and keep rearranging

our views until we get it right

the knife, as dearly as it is to a hunter's
mission, will not withhold its fury to
mutilate the body part of the hunter
involved with it at any careless or
innocent mishandling

my brokenness belittled my strength, i
delayed the answers i had for the
outsiders who questioned my fall, i stayed
very quiet with my wounded willingness
whose volume was still bigger than what i
had at first when putting my dreams together

fate and i are both writers, whenever i lay

out my dreams and dice them into acts

and scenes, fate will find the most suitable

fitting for them in the manuscript of the universe,

while the assembly into reality are

executed on and off agreement

more than a dozen times have i

mistakenly taken steps that shepherded

me to a barrel of truths, which upon

knowing, luminated the pitfalls and the

energy stations concealed in the

landscape of my dreams

to them, i was the one from the far end of the block,

noticeable and known to always run out of luck

but when my toils got served with a huge victory

they quickly cemented a new observation to my story

saying there was no appearance of me in

public without a book

giving credits to what i read as the

vessels i fetched the ideas to cook

the hands that pushed me hard into a
massive fall denied their involvement after
witnessing how shattered i became when i
hit the ground, they detailed their
innocence, but had their soles disfigured
in pain from trampling over the splinters of
me that continually caused them to bleed

the favourite place for relaxation and
deliberations that the gods have chosen in
all of their visits to my room is not the
spot that has their altar, i think they prefer
to loosen up and disregard protocols, i
even sense their absence sometimes, at
some fixed times of prayers

i straightened up my gun at the offender

who committed an offence that we all

agreed was a sin, same sin deeply and

hiddenly practiced within the inner circle

that i belonged, i secured the trigger with

my index finger and couldn't stop

wondering how punishments have made

the ignorant more governable, and sins

split one god into two contrasting deities

the ones who really think that special
miracles are always reserved and served to
them by their deity, have been shown the
grandest miracles happening outside the
demarcation of their camp, yet in the
compound of same universe

on the lucky chances i get to see you, i look

up to your face for that beautiful smile

that has penthouses of grin on both sides

of its route, where twinkle and beams and

soulfulness are poured into the magnetic

smile that always sweeps me off

certain muscles in my heart are reluctant

to respond whenever they are called up to

initiate forgiveness, until some distasteful

infection begins to attack them from the

surface due to lack of participation

in the playground of the gods, even if a
mistake is committed among the title
holders, the error will be packaged
and delivered to humans and it will still
make out a fine destiny without any
suspicion

religion has not been known to cast a kind

look on science or apologetic to its

followers whenever science, through

innocence, bursts any of its bubbles of myths

in love every colour sacrifices its hue to

become an accomplice to one pigment

the songs i often found on your lips

reminded me of my passion and my

demons when both were still young and

played together in their innocence

the beads that look like moles on the

surface of the pot of gold in my soul are

droplets of the gold itself that cooled

down late, but covered with skin to

hibernate the process

look closely into the chamber where peace

is manufactured, you will see where those

commonly hawked standards of dealing

with people are either bent or trashed just

for peace to have a seat

the ones who cast a long stare into the

deeps that their talents ask from them for

a headway, and never respond, are the

ones who turn deaf ears to the repeated

knocks of same talents, pretending to be

busy with other chores

the simple exercise of daily-counting

blessings by number always helps in

bringing attention to the tiny gratefulness

we bypass, which when put together can

wear the strength of a force capable of

capsizing a tonnage of disturbing sadness

what about the destinations i reached and
surpassed without the qualifications
required to attain them

what about the culture i disregarded and
the gods i unfollowed yet still earned my
salvation with my peace of mind intact

what about it

what about the shame and the expected
downfall that dissolved and lost their bond
on the same route that my dream
navigated unto fulfillments

the books i had been given enlightened

me more than the education i paid for,

nevertheless it was the costly education

that chiefly springboarded my diving into

the orbit where i met the ones who donated them

optimism was a priceless bracelet i

spotted in my low and i reached out and

grabbed it, the glow from it lit my way out

of the protracted darkness, and i've worn

it ever since, so much that it's become

inseparable with my identity but i wasn't

born with it

for my sanity, i do not attempt to draw a

difference between the consequences from

karma and the rejections i suffer from

attempting something new that will

eventually be cooked into a glory

those promises that arrived at the

doorstep to be delivered to me and got

retrieved were the ones that provided my

old demons with a resurrection to exhibit

their stunts

when life opened me to the options of its

scholarship, i opted for the one that took me to the sun

where i learnt how its rays were trained and toughened

before their engagement with light

dear friend, i've taken mine from the

prescription of advice i gave you but

about the dosage i recommended, i've not

devoured as much

the prescription said take two,

i took three,

four is for the gods and two is for humans

and this ailment already pushed me forth

to the interface of both

while i exist within a mindset that is older
than my age, i secretly search for the
playground from my childhood

and anytime i hear a familiar sound i
toe-tap my feet because that's the
universe alerting me of the arrival of my
kindred spirits

i placed my story side by side with things

widely celebrated and condemned, and i

saw that if i took same route and used

similar landmarks for my narrative, i would

jeopardize those crucial points that truly

defined me

mastering the art of solving complexities

rapidly only made my visits to hell more

frequent

i've played with many imaginations in my

consciousness so much that the

characters began to emerge in reality at

unexpected instances with memorized scripts

the conscience always collects my guilt

and dispatches it to my body language to

display, and more often than ever, it's

difficult to stop the trade because of the

efficiency of both units

after earning your trust, i reached deep

down within me and opened up my

concealed hurt and predicaments,

unknown to me that you just traded back

with a pseudo-trust and spoke to me from

a rehearsed script, and after extracting

what you needed to unseat my peace and

thwart my dreams, you removed your mask

there are always those fights that destroy

all other ammunitions and leave kindness

as the only weapon in the arsenal, never

hesitate to use it

i do believe in fears, i believe in their sizes
and threats but i also believe in the
temperature of the rooms we
accommodate them in our minds, the
freeze, the hot and the cold switches are
always at the keepers' control

even when i find it difficult to draw a clear
line between being liked very much and
being loved, i constructed a huge
contention where i see both as same
because the sacrifices launched from both
stations always leave me speechless, and
they do not always have different contents
or extents when unwrapped

the pain devastated me long before the

shame arrived to dig tunnels in my

countenance through which i conditioned

every good thing that came afterwards to

drown first and survive before believing

the sincerity in it

the reasons i made up on behalf of the

flying prey that missed my strikes came

from a part of me that managed my sanity

whenever expectations failed, not an

investigated report of what verily

transpired in the mind of the escaped target

9 798989 716302